Common Sense

FOR THE
21ST CENTURY

A CALL TO REINVEST IN
American Democracy

Dr. Paul J. McKenney, Ed.D, Colonel USA (Retired)

For information about this title or to order other books
and/or electronic media, contact the publisher:
Maine Freedom Press
mainefreedompress.com
info@mainefreedompress.com

ISBN: 979-8-9858037-0-9 (softcover)
979-8-9858037-1-6 (eBook)

Printed in the United States of America
Cover and Interior design: 1106 Design

Contents

Dedication

For my loving wife, Betsy, and our wonderful family.

Foreword

It is an honor for me to write the foreword for *Common Sense for the 21st Century: A Call to Reinvest in American Democracy*, the insightful new book by Dr. Paul J. McKenney, Ed.D, Colonel USA (Retired.) I have learned much over the years from my conversations with Paul, starting back when he and I first worked together at the United States Army War College in Carlisle, Pennsylvania, when I went there on detail from the Department of State after serving as the U.S. Ambassador to Brunei Darussalam from 2012-15.

Given my background in the U.S. Foreign Service, in which I served from 1985-2018, I tend to look at national security matters first of all from a diplomatic perspective, but In Paul's case, although he comes from an Army background, his view of national security is not centered on purely military concerns. He takes an exceptionally wide-ranging approach, drawing on his experiences not only in the Army, but also in the business world and in positions of elected municipal leadership. Repeatedly over the years, I have come away from conversations with Paul with some new insight, some innovative but practical way of looking at the problem. His ability to make such contributions reflects the many different kinds of problems that he has had real-world experience in working to solve.

Paul makes full use of this broad range of experiences in his book, focusing on a fundamental aspect of protecting U.S. national security: preserving the American way of life by ensuring the healthy functioning of U.S. democracy. He takes inspiration from Thomas Paine's classic *Common Sense*, the work that helped spark the American Revolution. Paul highlights a central point of Paine's *Common Sense*, that: "in a monarchy, the king is law, and, in a democracy, the law is king." Paul makes a compelling case that, in recent years, threats to America's core democratic principles, including the peaceful transfer of presidential power, have posed a profound danger to the republic. He urges principled leaders to work together across party lines to renew the American commitment to ensuring that the law remains the king. He argues that "in 2022, we face a similarly divided public as we did at our founding," and points out that "we must resist every attempt at appointing a king and reinvest in the bedrock principles of truth, freedom, and equal rights under the rule of law that underpin the very foundation of our representative republic."

Paul employs in his book the same basic organizing structure that Paine utilized in *Common Sense.* In Paul's first three chapters, he covers fundamental principles and traces the development of the American political system. In Chapter 1, Origins and Design of Government, he establishes the context, reviewing concepts of governance; the history of competition between autocratic and democratic rule; social contract theory as developed by Hobbes, Locke, and Rousseau and the influence of the theory on Paine; and the current era of renewed global competition between democracy and autocracy. Chapter 2, Overview of the American Political System, examines the aspects of the U.S. political system that make it distinctive. Paul focuses on the pivotal years in the 1770s and 1780s as the United States first won, and then consolidated, its independence from Great Britain. He writes that "the practice of a peaceful transfer of power following an election as well as military and civilian government allegiance to a constitution and the rule of law, have been the bedrock of the United States since 1789," when the U.S. Constitution came into effect. Chapter 3 considers "America's Political Class: Money vs. Merit. Paul notes that "even with a strong legal system, no democratic nation can long endure without an educated electorate and people of goodwill willing to protect the system from the corrosive forces of avarice and greed." He argues that "centrist political leaders who sought public office to serve the nation are retiring in large numbers and being replaced by extremists who refuse to compromise on any issue. This shift from a largely merit-based system that governed from the middle to a money-based system that props up extremists is a grave danger to the American political system."

In the latter three chapters and the Afterword, Paul looks at the current era and the future. Chapter 4 reviews the Present State of American Affairs. It focuses on the 2020 presidential elections and their aftermath in early 2021, arguing that "the legal framework surrounding our election system held fast in 2021, but the willingness of many elected and appointed officials at the highest level of government to overthrow the system, delegitimize the election, and support an insurrection was an astonishing, frightening, and unprecedented circumstance." Chapter 5, on Potential for America, examines "the centrality of a fair economic system, the importance of quality education, the need for vibrant communities, the necessity of a clean environment, and the fundamental requirement of security for all." The Conclusion, Chapter 6, argues that "all leaders of good character need to step up and do their part for society." The Afterword presents policy recommendations, such as national service, including non-military service, for all 18-year-olds; policies that support the health of citizens through better healthcare access, affordability, and a commitment to healthy communities; and educational policies that foster life-long learning networks.

In sum, Paul McKenney offers in *Common Sense for the 21st Century: A Call to Reinvest in American Democracy* an absorbing overview of the political challenges faced by the United States in the 21st Century and how Americans might meet these tests. He gives us an incisive, centrist perspective, grounded in decades of practical experience and reflection, on what it will take to restore the health of American political institutions.

Daniel Shields, Ambassador (ret.), is an Editorial Advisor at the Journal of Indo-Pacific Affairs. He has taught diplomacy courses and conducted diplomacy simulations at institutions including the University of Pennsylvania Carey Law School and the University of Michigan Ford School of Public Policy. The views expressed here are his own and do not necessarily reflect those of the Department of State or the U.S. Government.

Preface

Following the violent insurrection on the United States Capitol in Washington DC, on January 6, 2021, like most Americans, I found myself in a state of disbelief that a riotous mob had attempted to stop the peaceful transfer of presidential power for the first time in the history of the United States of America. Perhaps more astonishing was the fact that former President Trump had attempted a coup by inciting his supporters to march on the capitol. They did so with zeal, beating police officers and threatening the lives of elected leaders. Vice President Mike Pence and Speaker of the House of Representatives Nancy Pelosi were sought out by the insurrectionists to be murdered, while nearly 150 police officers were severely injured, and several police officers died as a result of the attack.

Shortly after the violence ended, Republican leaders in the United States House of Representatives and the United

States Senate rightly called out President Trump for his culpability. However, later that night after hiding from the insurrectionists, nearly two-thirds of the Republican members of the United States House of Representatives and a half-dozen Republican members of the United States Senate voted against the certification of President-elect Biden, without any evidence of voter fraud and with ample evidence to the contrary by Trump-administration election officials, courts at every level, and the United States Attorney General William Barr. This action against the certification of the presidential election, followed by more than a year of false election claims, has led many supporters of former President Trump to question the legitimacy of our representative democracy. In response, Republican legislators in many states have enacted voter-restriction laws, voter-suppression laws, and partisan election changes. These actions have continued the devolution of our representative democracy that started with the attempted coup on January 6, 2021. In this book, I will present why we must rise above the temptation to anoint a king, and why it is essential that we reinvest in our representative government with free and fair elections.

In the immediate aftermath of the January 6, 2021, insurrection, I decided to reread Thomas Paine's *Common Sense*, a book I had read in my college days some four decades ago. Paine wrote *Common Sense* in the early stages of the American Revolution to inspire colonists to shed the yoke of imperial rule. He encouraged American colonists to depose the British crown and establish a representative democracy, which they did after an eight-year revolution. I wrote my first draft of this book in February 2021 and revisited it only a year later, as I witnessed the unfortunate assault on our democratic republic continue unabated.

Now, in 2022, we have among us those who claim that the opposition party is their enemy rather than simply people who have different ideas regarding public policy. It is imperative that we get back to appropriate civil discourse in America; we need to be willing to agree to disagree on issues without animosity toward those who do not share our opinion on a particular topic. The emotional hype we hear from some political actors and media companies is tearing America apart, and our *real* competitors and adversaries such as Russia, China, N. Korea, Iran—and terrorist organizations—are benefiting from our disunity.

Throughout history, rulers of nations relied on support and consent from those who could keep them in power. The necessity for support is a requirement in all forms of governance, and it is especially relevant in representative democracies because leaders of democratic nations rely on the consent of the governed as an absolute requirement. In a democracy, the governed can vote to replace elected leaders if their leaders fail to meet expectations and the voters become dissatisfied. A healthy representative democracy relies on fair voting rights, an educated populace, and a citizenry that has faith in the electoral system, otherwise, representative democracy becomes untenable. The importance and absolute necessity of impartial, free, and fair elections at every level of government cannot be overstated.

In this book, I will revisit ideas that Thomas Paine promoted in *Common Sense* concerning representative democracy and why he believed it was the right path forward for the American colonists. Given our current circumstances, it is also necessary to update the ideas found in *Common Sense* and view them through a modern lens. My perspective is built upon a centrist, nonpartisan approach with extensive experience as a leader in the military, politics, and business. My roles as a husband, dad, and grandad reinforce and strengthen my motivation to do my part to help save our great country from all enemies foreign and domestic.

Introduction

The Englishman Thomas Paine published *Common Sense* in February 1776 to encourage colonial America to depose King George of Great Britain, claim their independence, and establish a representative democracy as a form of government. *Common Sense* became a rallying cry for the American Revolution as it laid out the important issues facing American colonists in the late 1770s. Paine made the case that government was a necessary requirement for any civil society, as evidenced by history. He also made the case that the English constitution and political system at that time was designed to subordinate America and treat colonists as second-class citizens. A central point of *Common Sense* is that, in a monarchy, the king is the law, and, in a democracy, the law is the king. This critical truth is the essence of *Common Sense,* as Paine called on colonists to depose the king and establish a representative democracy so that they may govern themselves.

Paine explained the weaknesses of a hereditary monarchy that survives by engaging in political patronage by favoring a political class based upon their support for the crown. He accurately identified that hereditary power often leads to incompetent leaders who are motivated by their zeal for personal power more than their concern for the common good. The idea that inherited power is somehow better than a system based upon merit is shown to be a foolish concept leading to bad outcomes, including unnecessary wars. This is as true today as it ever was, and it is proven out when we witness the world's autocratic leaders creating unnecessary conflicts. It is also common to find autocrats using proxies to cause trouble and start conflicts. In America we also have would-be autocrats who have wealth and assume that it is their birthright to be elected or who use their wealth to control elected leaders.

The state of affairs for America in 1776 was a divided public regarding how to move forward with respect to Great Britain. Many colonists wanted to stay loyal to King George and work things out, even though they had experienced the turmoil of taxation without representation, the forced quartering of British soldiers, and other insults to their dignity from the king and his government. A growing number of colonists believed that independence for America was an absolute necessity. Paine argued that independence was the only way to gain true freedom and escape the subservient position to the British monarchy.

In 2022, we face a similarly divided public as we did at our founding. My intent in this book is to share insights on why we must rise above the temptation to anoint a king or similar autocrat, on either the political right or the political left, and why we must reinvest in our representative government. Democratic governance is difficult, and there is no guarantee that it will survive the current assault from within and without. America is at an inflection point in our history where our republic is threatened by would-be autocrats and our freedoms are under assault from extremists who are undermining our democracy. Principled leaders must stand and be counted at this moment in history.

We must resist every attempt at anointing a king and reinvest in the bedrock principles of truth, freedom, and equal rights under the rule of law that underpin the very foundation of our representative democratic republic. The far right are engaged in a lie about the 2020 presidential election, and they seek to allow a former president and would-be tyrant to be anointed king of America. The far left seeks a socialist state where the federal government dictates far-reaching policies that would undermine the freedom and authority of states, municipalities, and individual citizens. Neither of these extreme positions are desirable, nor should we allow them to become a reality. America has succeeded because we have been governed largely from the center through a process of debate and compromise. To bring American governance back to the center, people of goodwill from both major political parties must agree to meet in the middle and defeat extremism.

This book is organized in a manner similar to that employed by Thomas Paine, with significant modifications to update the ideas for current times. I will endeavor to provide a modern perspective for the 21st century with insight developed through personal study, experience, and reflection of where America stands today. Every topic I touch upon will provide a cursory look at the relevant issues. Scholars in every field of social science and history have written volumes about these topics, and it is not my intent to rehash those great works. I will do my best to clearly state the facts that are in plain sight and make them accessible for all interested parties.

I will begin with sections on the origins and design of Government, followed by an overview of the American political system. Then I will consider America's political class; money vs. merit, demonstrating some weaknesses in our current system. I will explore the present state of American Affairs, as a way of sharing a perspective that may be useful to those who do not spend much time thinking about these issues. I will examine the potential for America, a country that offers so many possibilities, yet sometimes fails to adequately set the conditions for its citizens to achieve their potential. Finally, I will offer a brief review of some public-policy ideas that I believe could help us succeed moving forward.

Chapter 1

ORIGINS AND DESIGN
OF GOVERNMENT

Thomas Paine pointed out, and history confirms, that, as humankind came together in the long journey of creating civilizations, we had to learn how to cooperate with one another. Throughout history, for people to survive and thrive, societies had to be organized and governed in some manner. To achieve safety and stability, individuals and families empowered people in their community to organize rules and determine justice in order to make society work effectively. We refer to this concept as *governance*, and it has taken many forms in various countries and cultures across history. As a community developed, we can imagine leaders being selected formally or informally, and we can also imagine the stronger in a group, perhaps with a band of loyal followers, taking charge and dictating certain rules. In all societies throughout human history, some form of governance has taken hold, and, for better or worse, its leaders have organized how people in those societies lived and how they were governed.

Usually, governance took the form of kingdoms or monarchies, whereby a leader with an army of loyal followers ruled with absolute power. Often, the king, queen, czar, emperor, pharaoh, sultan, shah, grand ayatollah, Caesar, or whatever title they selected, ruled with absolute power, often crushing all opposition. Autocratic governance was common in most societies, and it achieved mixed results. Predominantly, the ruler became the law, but like most concepts, there are exceptions. In the ancient Greek city-state of Athens, during the 6th century BC, leaders developed an idea that became known as democracy, whereby free male citizens had a voice in selecting their leaders. This form of governance was designed to give select citizens the opportunity to choose their leaders directly by voting. Since that time, the competition between a form of autocratic rule and democratic rule has persisted, with autocratic rule being most common.

Regardless of the form of government, there is a concept in governance known as a *social contract* that implies rulers of governments have an unwritten social contract with the governed whereby citizens forego some freedoms and consent to be governed so that they can live in relative safety within a civilized society. The intellectual theory of a social contract between the governed and the government originated in the modern era with the English philosopher Thomas Hobbes (1588-1679) in his book *Leviathan*, published in 1651. Hobbes wrote *Leviathan* during the English civil war of 1642-1651. In *Leviathan*, he postulated that the state of nature for people without government was brutish, selfish, and uncivil. Hobbes favored a government led by a sovereign with absolute power, although he also presented an aristocracy or democracy as other possible forms of government. Hobbes held that the governed had no right to overthrow the sovereign and that the sovereign should act responsibly.

Following Hobbes' publication, new ideas regarding social-contract theory emerged during the Age of Enlightenment in the 17th and 18th centuries. John Locke (1632-1704), another English philosopher, presented a more optimistic view of the state of nature in his social-contract theory. In his *Second Treatise on Government*, first published in England in the late 1600s and later in America in 1773, Locke introduced the idea of the inalienable rights of man, a concept that was later incorporated into the American Declaration of Independence and eventually into the American governance model of a democratic republic. Jean-Jacque Rousseau (1712-1778), a Genevan Swiss philosopher, expanded on Locke's theory when he published *The Social Contract* in 1762. Rousseau theorized about why men would voluntarily give up some of their natural freedom and consent to be governed. He emphasized that when the government was no longer legitimately meeting its obligations, then the governed were justified in changing the government, by force if necessary. Thomas Paine (1737-1809) was likely intimately familiar with social-contract theory, including the philosophies of Hobbes, Locke, and Rousseau, and their ideas clearly informed his writings, including his seminal work, *Common Sense*, published in 1776.

In practice, a social contract between the governed and government means that rulers and governments must satisfy enough key constituencies to stay in power. However, if the ruler goes too far and angers a majority of his or her key constituencies, the governed may turn against the ruler and remove him or her from power. This can happen in an autocracy, an aristocracy, or a democracy. A modern-day example of this was when the autocratic Shah of Iran upset numerous key constituencies in Iran and lost their support.

In 1979, he was driven from power by a coalition of conservatives, moderates, and liberals, only to be replaced by a more oppressive autocrat who promised democracy and instead created a theocracy, an autocracy with a religious foundation, and placed himself in control as the grand ayatollah.

Tyranny is what is practiced by autocratic leaders as they gain power over people and attempt to remain in power against the will of the governed. Tyrannical leaders can emerge from the extreme left; such was the case of Vladimir Lenin and the Bolsheviks in the former Soviet Union in 1917 or the Chinese Communist Party in China that came to power in 1949 under the autocratic leader Mao Zedong. In both the communist Union of Soviet Socialist Republics and the communist People's Republic of China, the autocratic rulers killed millions of their own citizens in repressive crackdowns. Tyrannical leaders can also emerge from the extreme right; such was the case with the fascist leader Mussolini in Italy and the fascist leader Hitler and his Nazi party in Germany. In these regimes, the autocratic leaders also used repressive tactics to kill countless members of their own citizenry. There exists a dangerous ignorance and lack of understanding in America today about the power of autocracy and what can happen under an autocratic ruler.

The tendency toward tyranny and autocracy has a long history throughout the world, and it exists among some leaders in democracies who want to transform the democratic nations they rule into autocratic nations. Autocratic rulers assume different names, depending upon the society they rule. Kings, queens, and emperors ruled Europe for most of its history. With few exceptions, it has only been within the last one-hundred years that most of Europe transitioned to various democratic forms of governance. Several European nations are now parliamentary democracies, while some are constitutional monarchies, giving the monarch important head-of-state roles and duties. A few remain traditional monarchies, while some are republics, and some democracies are now moving toward autocratic rule.

The Middle East remains predominantly ruled by kings and emirs exercising absolute power to this day. In Asia, India, and South Korea are democracies, while Japan is a constitutional monarchy with an elected Prime Minister as head of government and an emperor as head of state. China is an autocracy ruled by a president who has the absolute power of a traditional emperor, while Russia is ruled by a president who wields the power of a czar in a kleptocracy, where a few oligarchs control most of the country's wealth and property. Each of the nations with autocratic leaders have powerful constituencies that support their respective rulers, even if it is not obvious at first glance. Autocrats consolidate power by destroying potential rivals and rewarding loyalists. Conversely, leaders of democratic governments must satisfy the general public in order to remain in power through elections.

In democratic nations, it is essential for leaders to have the consent of the governed. Democratic governments have a social contract with the people, and if elected leaders do not fulfill their part of the social contract, they become illegitimate and are voted out of office and replaced with new political leaders. In autocratic regimes, tyrants also have a social contract, but they often rule with impunity and answer only to select constituencies who prop them up by design, while crushing anyone who dares to challenge their power. Russia, China, Iran, and North Korea are chief examples of countries where tyrants rule without the genuine consent of their people. Several other leaders in democratic nations are currently flirting with autocratic rule, such as Erdogan of Turkey and Orban of Hungary.

Autocratic rulers in Russia, China, Iran, North Korea, and elsewhere are disruptive to a world order based upon rule of law and international norms that were built by western democracies following World War II. These disruptive powers continually challenge the rule of law and accepted international norms and practices throughout the world. In autocratic regimes, the king or equivalent ruler is the law, and in democracies, the law is the king. This fundamental difference between autocratic and democratic governance is key, so when democratic nations and their institutions are challenged by a would-be king or queen and their followers, it is essential to act to overcome such a threat lest people lose their hard-earned freedoms. Once freedom is lost, it is very difficult—often impossible—to recover.

Chapter 2

OVERVIEW OF THE AMERICAN POLITICAL SYSTEM

The American experiment in democratic governance began with the ideal principles penned in the Declaration of Independence, following a protracted attempt to reconcile with the British King George. After more than a decade of interference by King George, American colonial leaders in the 13 colonies sent delegates to convene the First Continental Congress in 1774. They discussed their relationship with the British monarchy and determined to work together in an attempt to resolve these issues. A year later, shortly after the Battles of Lexington and Concord in 1775 in the Commonwealth of Massachusetts, American colonial leaders convened the Second Continental Congress. They determined to protect their rights and freedoms, so they established the Continental Army in 1775 and appointed George Washington as its Commander in Chief.

A year later the Continental Congress met and officially adopted the Declaration of Independence on July 4, 1776, a document that was carefully vetted before being approved. This declaration ended any serious effort to reconcile with Great Britain. In late 1777, the Continental Congress created the Articles of Confederation as its first organizing documents that outlined how the colonies would work together. The Articles were officially adopted by the colonies in 1781 as the legal framework for America, and they were used until the United States Constitution was adopted in 1789 and established the democratic republic that still governs America in 2022. During the first several years of colonial governance, America was engaged in the Revolutionary War, which lasted eight long years, from 1775 to 1783. General Washington and the Continental Army, with significant help from France, finally defeated the British at Yorktown, Virginia.

Thomas Paine described an America in the 1770s where colonial leaders were at a crossroads in history. They were being oppressed and coerced by a British king who believed that American colonists owed him money and fealty because they were his subjects. King George sought to control and restrict the colonists' government and economy while treating them as second-class citizens by enacting laws without their input or consent. He was violating the unwritten social contract that had enabled the successful American colonial experience. This was a turning point in British-American relations. Thomas Paine encouraged American colonists to reject the king and claim their independence, which they eventually did.

Throughout the colonial era, American colonists applied English customs and laws to govern themselves. Municipalities, and the 13 original colonies, which later became the first 13 states, were originally organized with elected councils, and legislatures, while executives were appointed under British law. Once America became independent, colonial leaders wrote new charters and constitutions, and a democratic tradition of local, state, and federal representative governance was established. From 1781 to 1789, the Articles of Confederation were the legal governing documents that determined the relationship between the 13 separate colonies. This loose confederation proved to be insufficient to meet the needs of the times, and the independent colonies lacked cohesion. So, in 1789, using the Virginia constitution as a template, a new federal constitution with three branches of government was adopted.

The republic of the United States of America became a reality in 1789, with Congress being given substantial powers in Article I to make laws, raise and spend money, declare war, and oversee government. Article II authorized an executive branch to administer the law, and Article III authorized courts to interpret the law. The republic was to be governed as a representative democracy, with free and fair elections and a peaceful transfer of power following the counting of votes at every level of government. The constitution was designed to ensure that political power would be distributed among three co-equal branches of government, so that no one branch of government and no one person could consolidate power. The constitution also stipulated that political power would be dispersed and shared by federal and state governments. States and municipalities were free to write and ratify their own constitutions and charters respectively, so long as those legal documents did not contravene the federal constitution and law.

In the new republic, elected officials, appointed officials, civil servants, and members of the military swore allegiance to the constitution of the United States of America rather than to an individual or a monarch. State and local officials also swore allegiance to uphold the law in their respective constitutions and charters. This was the first time in world history that any military was subordinated to elected civilian leaders and all military members swore allegiance to a constitution, a legal framework, rather than an individual monarch. The practice of a peaceful transfer of power following an election as well as military and civilian government allegiance to a constitution and the rule of law have been the bedrock of the United States since 1789. These facts are of paramount importance and what makes America, the world's oldest democracy, exceptional and the most successful nation on Earth.

Chapter 3

AMERICA'S POLITICAL CLASS: MONEY VS. MERIT

When America declared independence from Great Britain and later adopted its constitution in 1789, colonists were hoping for a more perfect union based upon the rule of law, with competent elected political leaders who would respect their citizens and respond to the needs of the new nation. Knowing that human nature was flawed, the founders intentionally created checks and balances in the new constitutional framework. Still, even with a strong legal system, no democratic nation can long endure without an educated electorate and people of goodwill willing to protect the system from the corrosive forces of avarice and greed. America has been successful largely because good people have always been willing to step up when it mattered most, including during the insurrection of 2021. Today, in 2022,

America continues to be threatened by powerful forces that seek to destroy our democratic republic and replace it with an autocratic system that these forces believe they can control and benefit from. The current threat comes from the far right, which seeks a form of tyranny known as fascism, but a threat could also come from the far left in the future as an extreme form of socialism or communism. Many media outlets and unconstrained social media companies are sowing the seeds of doubt and discontent with a constant drumbeat of misinformation and emotional extremism under the guise of freedom of speech.

The desire for money and power seem to be the driving forces behind the assault on democracy. Powerful media moguls and their loyal puppets thrive by tearing apart social constructs and pitting neighbor against neighbor by promoting disinformation and misinformation to create an emotionally distressed population that acts out by attacking those with whom they disagree. Ignorant, misguided, and willfully corrupt political figures on the extreme right are using former President Trump's false claims of fraud in the 2020 election to get themselves elected. On the extreme left, there is a tendency to attack capitalism, corporations, and financially successful entrepreneurs as the ultimate evil. These loud extremist voices often emanate from those with little or no real education, experience, or understanding of actual governance. The extreme political figures spend their days raising money and gaining political support by making false statements and harming society. The rise of political extremism in America is destabilizing our society.

Those who perpetrate misinformation and discontent are getting richer and more powerful by sowing trouble and undermining our political system. Media moguls support incompetent, ignorant, and malicious candidates for public office and then manipulate them to sow further division. This is clearly evident in the relationship between former President Trump and far-right media outlets. Conservative political leaders who base their power on truth and a belief in a meritocracy are being sidelined by extremists who have taken over the political right. Centrist political leaders who sought public office to serve the nation are retiring in large numbers, and they are being replaced by extremists who refuse to compromise on any issue. This shift from a largely merit-based system that governed from the middle to a money-based system that props up extremists is a grave danger to the American political system.

Chapter 4

PRESENT STATE OF AMERICAN AFFAIRS

In America, the social contract between the governed, who willingly consent to elected political leaders, and the government, is essential to enable effective democratic governance. Consent is based upon trust and confidence that people have in their political leaders and government institutions. To achieve consent, it is necessary for political leaders to be truthful and committed to the rule of law while abiding by appropriate social and political norms that advance the well-being of all citizens. America will remain a great nation only if political leaders from both major political parties respect the citizenry and hold themselves to high standards of personal and professional integrity. It is incumbent on all political leaders in America to live up to the highest standards of ethical behavior. It is also essential that citizens are well informed so that they can hold political leaders accountable. We need politicians to turn away from extremism, engage with one another peacefully, and find healthy compromise bound by a commitment to public service. For too long, extremists on the right and the left, along with their respective allies in the media, have taken society down a dangerous and destructive path of division.

In the beginning of 2021, 245 years after Thomas Paine inspired our forefathers to claim their independence and forsake a king, we found ourselves in an unfortunate and uncertain situation. For the first time in the history of our republic, an American president and his most ardent followers were unwilling to acknowledge the results of a free and fair presidential election. Many misinformed and some willfully seditious actors tried to prevent the peaceful transfer of presidential power by engaging in an unlawful and deadly insurrection on January 6, 2021. Worse, a majority of elected leaders from the Republican party in the U.S. House of Representatives and a substantial number in the U.S. Senate refused to acknowledge the election results, and they willingly opposed the certification of the federal presidential election of 2020. They attempted to make a former president king and make their king the law, in direct contravention of our democratic system, where the law is king. This action, if successful, would have ended the experiment of the United States of America as a democratic republic and turned our country into an autocratic state ruled by a tyrant.

Fortunately, in the United States, elections take place at the municipal and county level and are certified at the state level based upon state laws. Votes are cast and counted according to federal and state laws, so that voting is fair and legal, and no group or individual is disenfranchised. This process makes it difficult but not impossible to corruptly overturn an election. The 2020 election relied on well-established rules and reliable voting machines that were backed up by paper ballots for verification, and, according to federal election officials appointed by the former president, including his Attorney General, it was the most reliable and fair election in United States history. Every assessment and recount ended with the same legitimate result, and every court challenge led to the same electoral outcome. The twice-impeached former president lost the election fair and square, yet he and his key supporters continue to undermine our democracy by falsely claiming that the election was stolen.

The legal framework surrounding our election system held fast in 2021, but the willingness of many elected and appointed officials at the highest levels of government to overthrow the system, delegitimize the election, and support an insurrection was an astonishing, frightening, and unprecedented circumstance. States' rights and a voting system that is decentralized from the federal government proved essential, and the election was objectively certified based upon actual results. This decentralization and the unwillingness of states to illegally disenfranchise voters was an essential safeguard for the continuation of the republic. These safeguards are currently under assault by the former president and his followers as his political lackeys in many states across the country engage in voter-suppression tactics, in an attempt to gain political advantage in future elections. The danger of these actions by unethical actors is significant and could undermine the continuation of our democratic republic.

Many of the battleground states where the former president lost and where his political party has control of state legislatures are now establishing voter-suppression laws that favor their party in the next election and allow them to overturn election results if they do not like the outcome. An objective look at this current attempt reveals a disturbing trend. America has become increasingly polarized in the past few decades, and dark money has become an ever-increasing menace to our political system. In the early 1990s, twenty-six states had an elected U.S. Senator from each major political party. That situation gradually shifted, so that by 2020, only six states had an elected Senator from each major political party.

The problem with this trend is that it makes cooperation and collaboration among elected leaders from different political parties much less likely. The result is that political parties tend to push their own agendas when in power and focus on their own party's constituents rather than serving the nation as a whole. If this polarization continues unabated, our political system may collapse under its own partisan weight. We have the potential to recover from these divisions and the latest acts of sedition they engender, but only if people of goodwill from both major political parties fully engage with honesty and integrity and take actions to protect democracy by creating minimum federal standards that safeguard voting rights.

Chapter 5

POTENTIAL FOR AMERICA

To understand America's potential, we need to review a few key topics that impact everyone, beginning by highlighting some key facts from our history. This will be followed by an overview of human motivation from a humanistic-psychology perspective, because motivation is what ultimately drives human behavior. Then the topics of economics, education, community, environment, and security will be discussed in the context of how they fit into the future of America. These are the fundamental areas where government has the duty and responsibility to act and use the law to support the best interests of its citizens. The fundamental social contract between the government and the governed must be strengthened in America for our nation to endure.

The United States of America has always been a country of great promise and possibilities. Since its fledgling beginning in the 1770s, followed by an eight-year revolution from 1775 to 1783, a loose confederation of colonies from 1781 until 1789, and, finally, a ratified constitution in 1789 that established our present republic with elected leaders serving at all levels of government, America has overcome every obstacle and challenge she has encountered. The foundational institution of slavery was eventually eliminated, and two insurrections were defeated, one to maintain slavery in the 1860s and another to overthrow our democracy and install a dictator in 2021. All internal and external challengers who sought to overthrow our republic were vanquished. Some of our most ardent enemies in the past are now our closest allies and friends, while new adversaries are challenging America's dominance on the world stage and undermining our democratic institutions. America still has great potential, but we need quality leaders who are willing to take on and defeat those who would seek our demise.

The United States and the world are at an inflection point in 2022, and our republic is again threatened from both internal and external adversaries. Nations, like individuals, never quite reach equilibrium—they are either moving forward or moving backward. The history of America and especially the history of the nearly eight decades since World War II have ushered in unprecedented change in the world, and some of these changes have caused unforeseen disruptions to everyday life, resulting in both positive and negative unintended consequences. Understanding these issues and what they mean moving forward will require a brief review of the centrality of a fair economic system, the importance of quality education, the need for vibrant communities, the necessity of a clean environment, and the fundamental requirement of security for all. However, before we look into these topics, it will be helpful to review human motivation from a holistic humanistic-psychology perspective.

Humanistic psychologist Abraham Maslow (1908-1970) studied human motivation and behavior to understand what causes people to behave the way they do. He published his *Theory of Human Motivation* in 1943, and it still stands as one of the most important theories of human motivation ever developed. His primary findings became known as Maslow's Hierarchy of Needs, and, although Maslow's work does not explain all human behavior, it does provide great insight into what motivates people. According to Maslow, the needs that motivate people are interrelated and fall into three broad categories: Basic, Psychological, and Self-fulfillment.

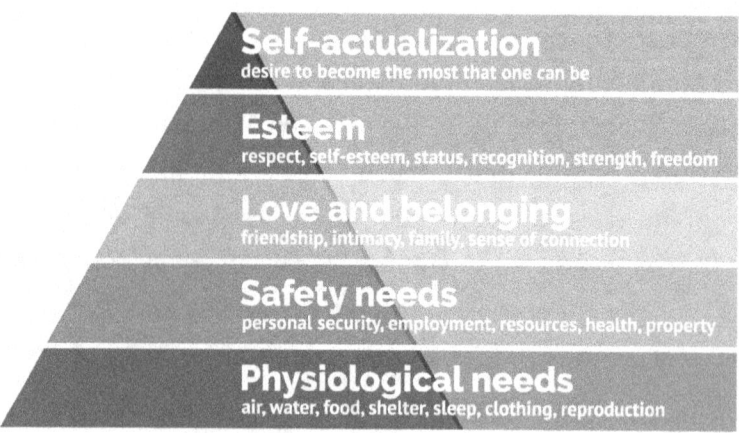

Basic needs are both physiological and safety related based upon our innate drive for survival. Basic physiological needs include air, water, food, sleep, health, and shelter. These fundamental survival needs are closely related to safety needs that include personal security, emotional security, financial security, and personal well-being. Until these basic needs are met, it is impossible to move forward with living in any meaningful way, which may explain why much of the world, including significant parts of America, are currently in turmoil. When basic needs cannot be met in acceptable ways, people find alternative ways, such as crime and gangs, to fulfill their basic requirements. A rise in crime threatens the basic safety needs of people and leads to less secure circumstances and a downward spiral in the social fabric of families and communities.

Following basic physiological and security needs, the next level of needs Maslow identified were psychological. These include belongingness and love needs as well as esteem needs. He concluded that people are social beings in need of love, friendship, family, and intimacy. We have two levels of esteem needs, according to Maslow. The lower level of esteem needs includes a need for respect from others such as status, recognition, attention, and a feeling of accomplishment. Examples of higher-level esteem needs are self-respect, mastery, competence, and freedom. When people live in circumstances that make these needs difficult to fulfill in conventional ways, they tend to find unconventional and often inappropriate ways to fulfill their needs. It is easy to see that, when important needs are not met, families and communities can devolve, and that can lead to a breakdown of important social norms in society.

At the top of the hierarchy of needs, when all other needs are fulfilled, we have self-actualization and, finally, transcendence. Self-actualization is about achieving one's innate potential. It may mean partnering with a mate, parenting, pursuing important goals, as well as utilizing and developing inherent talents. The final stage of development that Maslow explored later in his life was the concept of transcendence, dedicating one's self to a higher cause.

This brief overview of humanistic psychology and human motivation is meant to set the stage for the ensuing discussion. By understanding fundamental humanistic psychology that motivates people and drives their behavior, we can develop an intellectual framework and apply it to our understanding of what has happened and is happening in our society and in the broader world. Economics, which is fundamentally connected to all human needs, will be our starting point.

Economic and financial well-being are essential to live in a modern society, yet this topic is confusing for many because it is not widely understood in a meaningful way. To better comprehend our current economy, which is based upon a capitalist economic model, it is useful to look into history. Adam Smith (1723-1790) an English political philosopher and economist wrote *The Wealth of Nations*, first published in 1776, as a way of helping people understand how wealth is created and how economies actually work. Extrapolating from his seminal work, we can understand in a fundamental way how the modern capitalist system came to be and, more importantly, why it works the way it does. Wealth on an individual level or in a nation is largely determined by how several important factors come together. These factors include labor, the cost of raw goods, the creation of something customers will purchase, and the demand for finished products and services.

To illustrate how this works in practice, we will use a simple example. Let's assume a woman named Sue wants to be in the business of selling pizza. She can set up shop and purchase the necessary ingredients, such as tomato sauce, eggs, flour, cheese, etc.... and then add her productive labor to create pizza. Then she can sell the pizza to interested customers. This simple example shows how products combined with labor and ingenuity can create something of value. By purchasing the ingredients from a lower-cost supplier, Sue can increase her profit margin and make more pizza to sell. This is a simple example, but it is fundamentally how business works and how profits are made. Products and services are created by combining ingredients, labor, and ingenuity to meet the needs and wants of customers. As demand increases, prices go up, and then more supply follows, usually through competition, until some equilibrium is met between supply and demand, leading to prices eventually stabilizing.

In a capitalist economy, people are motivated to create products and services to fulfill wants and needs that customers desire. They then sell the products or services for a profit, and they ultimately create income and wealth in the process. This earned wealth is taxed by governments and supports public services and institutions in numerous ways. Those who are willing to invest their own money and labor into business enterprises can benefit from business success and share in wealth creation. Risk is a fundamental factor in business creation, and a large percentage of new businesses fail in their first few years; most successful business people have experienced previous business failures. Sometimes even older, well-established businesses fail because their product or service becomes obsolete or new competitors win market share. Business creation and development is inherently risky, so most people choose to be employees rather than business owners, however, they can still participate in business success by investing and gaining some ownership interest through the purchase of stock in business enterprises.

A major challenge in our capitalist economy is the constant and highly disruptive changes taking place that are often destabilizing to people who require a steady income. However, this constant change is a normal and expected outcome of the competitive nature of our economic system. It actually makes the system more efficient and productive as superior products and services replace inferior products and services. Competition is a necessary disrupter that drives innovation and creativity. The particular secret to American business success is freedom and limitless possibilities for those who are willing to take risks and test their ideas in the marketplace. The competitive nature of capitalism also means that a reasonable regulatory regime is necessary to keep the system fair and safe. Too much regulation slows the system down and stifles innovation, while too little regulation allows greedy, unscrupulous actors to prey upon innocent victims.

A carefully balanced regulatory structure is essential to protect workers, the public, the community, and the environment, but it is difficult to achieve and requires constant monitoring and regular adjustments. Unbridled capitalism leads to greed that tends to trample on the rights of others, but honest profits earned in an ethical manner should be celebrated and encouraged. The capitalist economic system becomes problematic when corporate welfare is practiced and when workers lack the knowledge and skills to adapt to changing economic conditions that inevitably occur. Disruptions occur due to business cycles, inventions, innovation, government policy changes, and unforeseen events such as war and natural disasters. The biggest and most disruptive change for economies is sudden, massive innovation, or a paradigm shift in how the economy functions.

Globally we are currently experiencing a paradigm shift in the economy due to the advent of what economists call the "fourth industrial revolution." However, this economic shift is uneven and therefore can be destabilizing due to globalization. In each of the previous three industrial revolutions in world history, the nations who were able to catch the coming economic wave eventually became a dominant power. Unfortunately, workers often suffer during these industrial revolutions because of the resulting economic transformations taking place. The first industrial revolution was in the latter half of the 1700s, around the time of the American Revolution. It was an age of increasing mechanization and a move away from hand work toward machine work. This was quite disruptive for those whose work was replaced by equipment and machinery.

The second industrial revolution began in the latter half of the 1800s and was equally disruptive and transformational. The changes included the discovery of electricity, oil, gas, and chemical synthesis as well as the development of trains and the invention of the automobile. One hundred years later, the third industrial revolution arrived in the late 1900s with the invention of electronics, tele-communications, and the computer. Finally, the fourth industrial revolution is upon us in the early 21st century, driven by the internet, quantum computing, and artificial intelligence. Each industrial revolution has advanced society in countless ways, but each has also included an economic paradigm shift that brought about massive economic disruptions that displaced many workers who had spent their careers in fields that literally ceased to exist in a short time period. For these reasons, quality holistic interdisciplinary education is a necessity in the modern era to minimize the negative consequences of inevitable economic transformations.

Education is the most fundamental area in need of constant investment and innovation, because it serves as the great equalizer in a free society. It is the lifeblood of any nation, as it equips the population with the necessary knowledge, skills, and abilities to be successful in an ever-changing economic landscape. Versatility and adaptability are essential qualities for both children and adults in order to succeed in the modern age. Lifelong learning has become a necessity for all people, and it can be encouraged and enhanced with great educators, appropriate schooling opportunities, and excellent libraries providing access to information. When quality interdisciplinary education begins at an early age and continues throughout adulthood, the most disruptive aspects of capitalism can be softened, as citizens will be better equipped to adapt to changes that will inevitably occur in an innovative economy.

Along with an efficiently regulated economy and a high-quality educational system that serves everyone, a successful society requires healthy, vibrant communities where the well-being of citizens is the first priority of government. This means safe neighborhoods free of crime, access to quality, affordable healthcare, well-constructed and well-maintained infrastructure, walkable neighborhoods and parks, excellent public facilities, public-transportation options, and access to the basic necessities of life, including quality food options. These attributes of healthy communities are readily available in neighborhoods with higher-income earners, but they are less common in areas where lower-income earners reside—and that must change. The lack of adequate resources that plagues lower-income areas presents a serious problem for major segments of society throughout America in urban and rural areas alike, where people cannot meet some of their basic human needs. As a result, these populations often feel ignored, and they fall prey to greedy grifters, media outlets, and social media sites who abuse those in need with grievance politics. In addition to the importance of educational opportunities, vibrant communities also require a clean environment.

Irrespective of one's particular opinion regarding climate change and what percentage is natural versus man-made, it is not a controversial fact that clean air and clean water are absolutely essential for life on Earth. So, if we take our responsibility as stewards of Mother Earth seriously from a spiritual, religious, or secular perspective, then we must act to ensure that the air is clean, the water is pure, and the environment is protected. We need to clean up the damage done and do a better job of preventing unnecessary pollution moving forward. Environmental degradation is going to occur when humankind interacts with nature, but if we use our inherent powers to think and act ethically, then we can minimize damage that occurs and make the world a better place for all to enjoy. The excuses that people make for the destruction they cause needs to stop, and we must put our best efforts forward for the benefit of future generations.

Finally, meeting the basic needs for physical and emotional security on an individual and societal level must improve.

Keeping the American people safe and feeling secure is the most important responsibility of government. Without security, nothing else matters. Communities require adequate policing and social services that help those in need. Citizens in neighborhoods and communities throughout America have a basic right to feel and be safe. Justice matters and needs to be a top priority for all elected and appointed officials at all levels of government.

On the national level, the most fundamental responsibility of government is to keep Americans safe from all enemies, foreign and domestic. There are enemies in America and abroad who would gladly destroy our constitutional republic, and some of them are being convinced by the big lie promoted by the twice-impeached former president and his key followers and loyal media outlets to undermine our society. Former President Trump and his followers must be prevented from overthrowing our democratic republic, and the rule of law and truth must prevail, with swift and severe justice for those who attempt to unlawfully undermine our republic. Foreign adversaries who wish us ill, including Russia, China, North Korea, and Iran, as well as non-state terrorist organizations, must be confronted with all the appropriate levers of power we and our allies can bring to bear against them. Domestically, according to our own FBI, we have destructive forces among us who irrationally fear that immigrants and minorities are taking away their franchise. Additionally, we must guard against a trend on the far left to take advantage of the instability these circumstances create to launch their own takeover.

Chapter 6

CONCLUSION

America has great potential and limitless possibilities. To achieve our potential, we must recognize that we are at a pivotal time in history and our democratic republic is in grave danger from real foreign and domestic threats. On January 6, 2021, we experienced an attack on our government that was led by a president and his political allies in the United States Congress. This failed coup was fueled by a disproven lie regarding the outcome of the 2020 presidential election, and it has undermined confidence in our electoral system. We must reinvest in our democratic republic by holding insurrectionists—both the foot soldiers and their leaders—fully accountable.

The attempted coup revealed numerous underlying systemic problems that must be expeditiously addressed in law and followed up with appropriate policies and concrete actions. We are in the midst of a fourth industrial revolution that is destabilizing our society, as many workers are being displaced because they lack the requisite skills to adapt to a changing economic landscape. We need an educational system that is sufficiently adaptive for a workforce that is unprepared for the coming changes. The economic paradigm shift and its resulting changes in our economy can and must be harnessed to make our communities stronger. Additionally, we must rapidly address the unprecedented changes in our climate by teaching everyone the importance of being good stewards of our world and by taking necessary steps to improve environmental outcomes. Finally, we must attend to the security needs across society to guarantee safe neighborhoods throughout America, along with safe and secure borders. Criminals at all levels of society must be held accountable, and adversaries must understand that America will defend its interests from any potential foe.

At this inflection point in history, America needs mature, stable leaders who place the citizens of our great nation before their own personal interests. All leaders of good character need to step up and do their part to improve society. Together, people of goodwill can smooth out our economic transformation, build resilience into our educational system, enhance and strengthen our communities, take care of our environment, and protect our society from all enemies, foreign and domestic. It is my sincere hope that we can come together and work toward a bright and prosperous future for all people of goodwill in the United States of America and that we can help shape the world to achieve positive outcomes for humanity.

Afterword

POLICY RECOMMENDATIONS
FOR ELECTED LEADERS

As I consider the challenges facing our society and the world writ-large, it seems appropriate to offer some suggestions that may be useful for competent elected leaders to address in policy. If we consider the key topics of the economy, education, community, environment, and security discussed above, we can address many of the important issues relating to these topics with three major lines of effort. The lines of effort that cover the key topics are national service, healthcare access, and lifelong learning. These lines of effort will require numerous subordinate and well-coordinated lines of operation. Significant components of the necessary framework to address these societal problems already exist, but they need an overarching strategy to connect them and coordinate synergistic outcomes.

There has been significant discussion over many years regarding the potential value of national service, and several prominent leaders, including retired General Stanley McCrystal, have committed themselves to this endeavor. We currently have a Selective Service program in place that requires 18-year-old males to register, so that, in a national emergency, the nation may call these men to military service. My recommendation is to expand the Selective Service to all 18-year-olds, male and female, and to modify its operation and purpose. Offer all 18-year-olds in America an opportunity for a physical and mental-aptitude assessment and interest inventory when signing up for the Selective Service. The young people would then have an idea of their aptitude and interests that they may use to volunteer for various opportunities with various pay and benefit options.

For example, one young person may qualify for military service as an aircraft mechanic, while another may qualify for and have an interest in further education to become a nurse, and a third may want to volunteer for an opportunity focused on the environment. The idea is that all young people could get a baseline assessment of aptitudes and interests and have associated opportunities that open up possibilities for them. All national service should come with pay and educational opportunities, including higher-education benefits that advance future possibilities. These voluntary positions could be part-time or full-time, and they would undoubtedly help focus young people in productive directions. Preliminary basic training could include general civics lessons along with specialty education for a chosen position or field. This type of national service could help fill vital gaps in our society and help young volunteers get a running start in life.

A second policy idea is to focus on the absolute necessity of healthy citizens. This is not a new idea, however, it is an area that needs greater focus by policy-makers. Maslow identified health as a basic need for good reason. Anyone who has experienced serious health issues understands that, when you are sick, everything else becomes impossible. Access to affordable, quality healthcare, healthy food choices, and places for people to relax and play are vital for good health. We can achieve these outcomes by creating policies that support access, affordability, and a commitment to healthy communities.

Finally, in an advanced society, it is essential to have educational frameworks in place that offer quality learning opportunities from preschool through a person's lifetime. We already have a vast educational network of schools, colleges, and libraries. We need to harness these institutions and coordinate them in a manner that fulfills society's needs by creating learning networks, skill-development opportunities, and information access universally available in an integrated manner. Lifelong-learning networks across the spectrum of community colleges, public and private universities, and libraries would go a long way to supporting a public in need of constant knowledge and skill development in an ever-changing economy.

Public policy should focus on setting conditions that strengthen and protect the American democratic republic. The most fundamental action that will support the above ideas is to ensure full participation by our citizenry by setting minimum federal rules for electoral certification, congressional redistricting, and voting rights. Government works best when it focuses on well-formulated policy-setting conditions that support freedom while protecting citizens from the avarice and greed of some politicians and some corporate leaders. We do best when we work together based upon the principles of truth and freedom.

Bibliography

Abraham Maslow, *Theory of Human Motivation*,
  Start Publishing, Summit, NJ 2012

Adam Smith, *The Wealth of Nations*, Heritage
  Illustrated Publishing 2014

Captivating History, *American History: A Captivating Guide
  to the History of the United States of America* 2020

Jean-Jacque Rousseau, *The Social Contract,* Digireads.com 2009

John Locke, *Two Treatises of Government and a Letter
  Concerning Toleration,* Digireads.com 2015

Moses I. Finley, *Democracy Ancient and Modern,* Rutgers
  University Press, New Brunswick, NJ 1996

Sterling Education, *Everything You Always Wanted to Know About
  American History*, Sterling Education, Boston, MA 2022

Thomas Hobbs, *Leviathan*, Digireads.com 2014

Thomas Paine, *Common Sense*, Coventry House
  Publishing, Dublin, OH 2016

https://www.usa.gov/history

Declaration of Independence 1776

United States Constitution 1789

About the Author

Dr. Paul J. McKenney EdD is a retired U.S. Army Colonel who served 30 years as an aviation officer in all components of the Army, including the Regular Army, National Guard, and Army Reserve. He served in assignments across the United States, Germany, Canada, Saudi Arabia, and Afghanistan. He is an Excellent Graduate of the Air War College and a Distinguished Graduate of the U.S. Army War College. He led a Canadian Army team in Afghanistan, served as Director of Facilitation for strategic war games at the Center for Strategic Leadership and as Course Director for Strategic Leadership in Current and Future Warfare at the United States Army War College. He is a Senior Lecturer in Law at the University of Pennsylvania Carey Law School, focused on strategic leadership and national-security issues.

Paul earned a baccalaureate degree in humanistic studies with an emphasis in world studies, philosophy, and history. He holds master's degrees in public administration and strategic studies, and a doctorate in educational leadership. Paul served as an elected municipal leader as Chairman of the Town Council of Cape Elizabeth, Maine. He also served as president of the Greater Portland Council of Governments (GPCOG), Maine, overseeing collaboration of governance issues across 26 municipalities and as chairman of the region's federally established Economic Development District. In these roles, he and his dedicated colleagues established the Seven Principles of Sustainability in 2008 that were universally adopted by GPCOG's 26-member municipalities. This focus on principles as a foundation for governing led to steady growth in the regional economy, stronger communities, and a cleaner environment for all to enjoy.

As a business leader, Paul serves as the president and CEO of a wealth-management firm and has 30 years of experience as a leader in the financial-services industry. He holds designations as a Certified Financial Planner®, and Accredited Investment Fiduciary® along with numerous securities licenses. As a community volunteer, Paul served on the executive board of Pine Tree Council Boy Scouts of America and as president of the council's National Eagle Scout Association chapter. Paul believes in active constructive engagement by all. He espouses an independent political perspective based upon facts, where all parties practice reasonable compromise and consideration of others.